WORLD WAR II CHRONICLES

FROM D-DAY TO V-E DAY

DWIGHT JON ZIMMERMAN,
MILITARY HISTORY CONSULTANT

BY JULIE KLAM

Published by Smart Apple Media, 1980 Lookout Drive, North Mankato, Minnesota 56003

Produced by Byron Preiss Visual Publications, Inc.

Library of Congress Cataloging-in-Publication Data

Klam, Julie.

From D-Day to V-E Day / by Julie Klam.

v. cm. — (World War II chronicles; bk. 5)

Contents: The war in the east — D-Day — Operation Cobra — The commanders — Exploiting the U.S. First Army breakout

from Normandy — Operation Dragoon: the liberation of the south of France — Liberation of Paris — Battle of the Hürtgen

Forest — Operation Market-Garden — The liberation of Italy — Battle of the Bulge — Capture of the Remagen bridge —

Rhine river crossings — Patton's Third-Army drive through Germany to Czechoslovakia — Liberation of concentration

camps: the Holocaust — The drive to Berlin — The link-up of American and Soviet forces at Torgau, Germany — V-E Day —

Epilogue: war crimes trials at Nuremburg and the Marshall Plan.

ISBN 1-58340-191-1

1. World War, 1939-1945—Campaigns—Western Front—Juvenile literature. 2. World War, 1939-1945—Campaigns—

Eastern Front—Juvenile literature. [1. World War, 1939-1945—Campaigns—Western Front. 2. World War, 1939-1945—

Campaigns—Eastern Front.] I. Title.

D756 .K53 2002

940.54'2—dc21   2002017702

First Edition   •

2 4 6 8 9 7 5 3 1

CONTENTS:

INTRODUCTION

+ (opposite): Adolf Hitler addresses the Reichstag.

World War II was the greatest conflict of the 20th century. Fought on every continent except Antarctica and across every ocean, it was truly a "world war." Like many other wars, over time it evolved. Modern technology and strategic advancements changed the rules of combat forever, allowing for widespread attacks from the air, the ground, and the sea.

For the Chinese, the war began in 1931, when Japan invaded northeastern China. When Germany invaded Poland in 1939, Europeans were dragged into the fray. Americans did not enter World War II until December 7, 1941, when Japan attacked Pearl Harbor, Hawaii.

World War II pitted two sides against each other, the Axis powers and the Allied countries. The main Axis nations were Germany, Japan, and Italy. The Axis powers were led by Chancellor Adolf Hitler, the head of the Nazi Party in Germany; Premier Benito Mussolini, the head of the Fascists in Italy; and Japan's Emperor Hirohito and the military government headed by Prime Minister Hideki Tojo. The Allies included Britain, France, the Soviet Union, China, and the United States. The leaders of the Allies were Britain's Prime

+ Benito Mussolini

+ Hirohito

Winston Churchill

Minister Winston Churchill, who had replaced Neville Chamberlain in 1940; General Charles de Gaulle of France; the Soviet Union's Marshal Josef Stalin; China's Generalissimo Chiang Kai-shek; and Franklin Delano Roosevelt, the president of the United States. The two sides clashed primarily in the Pacific Ocean and Asia, which Japan sought to control, and in the Atlantic Ocean, Europe, and North Africa, where Germany and Italy were trying to take over.

World War II finally ended in 1945, first in Europe on May 8, with Germany's total capitulation. Then, on September 2, the Japanese signed the document for their unconditional surrender after the United States had dropped two atomic bombs on Japan. World War II left 50 million people dead and millions of others wounded, both physically and mentally.

The war encompassed the feats of extraordinary heroes and the worst villains imaginable, with thrilling triumphs and heartrending tragedies. *From D-Day to V-E Day* covers the final battles that led to the end of the war in Europe.

Charles de Gaulle

✝ Josef Stalin

✝ Chiang Kai-shek

✝ (right): Franklin Delano Roosevelt

Map of German Conquests

Legend:
- Germany (1939)
- Axis Occupied Territory (1942)
- Italy and Its Territories
- Treaty with Axis
- Allied Powers
- Allied Protectorates
- Neutral Countries
- Vichy France and Territories

NORWAY

FINLAND

SWEDEN

ESTONIA

North Sea

Baltic Sea

LATVIA

DENMARK

LITHUANIA

UNION OF
SOVIET SOCIALIST REPUBLICS

IRELAND

UNITED
KINGDOM

EAST
PRUSSIA

THE
NETHERLANDS

BELGIUM

GERMANY

POLAND

*Atlantic
Ocean*

LUXEMBOURG

FRANCE

SLOVAKIA

SWITZERLAND

HUNGARY

VICHY
FRANCE

YUGOSLAVIA

ROMANIA

Black Sea

PORTUGAL

Adriatic Sea

BULGARIA

SPAIN

ITALY

ALBANIA

TURKEY

SPANISH
MOROCCO

GREECE

SYRIA

IRAQ

MOROCCO

Mediterranean Sea

PALESTINE

ALGERIA

TUNISIA

TRANS-
JORDAN

LIBYA

EGYPT

SAUDI
ARABIA

The Pacific Campaign

ALASKA

U.S.S.R.

MONGOLIA

MANCHURIA

CHINA

KOREA

JAPAN

TIBET

INDIA

BURMA

HONG KONG

FRENCH INDOCHINA

THAILAND

BORNEO

DUTCH EAST INDIES

NEW GUINEA

AUSTRALIA

ALEUTIAN ISLANDS

ATTU, KISKA
May-Aug. 1943

Doolittle Raid
Apr. 18, 1942

MIDWAY
June 1942

PEARL HARBOR
Dec. 7, 1941

OKINAWA
April-June 1945

IWO JIMA
Feb.- March 1945

THE PHILIPPINES
Oct. 1944-June 1945

SAIPAN, GUAM & TINIAN
June-Aug. 1944

TARAWA
November 1943

GUADALCANAL
Aug. 1942-Feb. 1943

U.S. aircraft carrier
Battle
Allied advance
Japanese possession before Dec. 7, 1941
Japanese conquest after Dec. 7, 1941
Limit of Japanese expansion

THE WAR IN THE EAST

On August 13, 1942, Soviet Marshal Josef Stalin drafted a memorandum to British Prime Minister Winston Churchill and President Franklin D. Roosevelt criticizing their decision not to invade Western Europe in 1942.

In the memo, Stalin emphasized the Allies' need to relieve the pressure on the Eastern Front (U.S.S.R.). Stalin pressed his allies to open a second front in Western Europe against Hitler. Responding to the sieges of Leningrad and Stalingrad, the Soviet Union was locked in major battles against the German invaders, whereas the British were fighting a much smaller German army in northern Africa, and the American army had yet to engage the Germans.

> ## MEANWHILE IN THE PACIFIC
> In August 1942, U.S. Navy and Marine forces battle the Japanese on and around the southwestern Pacific island of Guadalcanal.

Stalin would deliver many memos before the second front was finally opened with the American, British, and Canadian invasion of Normandy, France, on June 6, 1944.

The siege of Leningrad lasted about 900 days. Leningrad (now called St. Petersburg) was named after Lenin, the founder of the Soviet Union. The city is located on the Karelian Isthmus between the Gulf of Finland and Lake Ladoga near the southeast border of Finland. The attack on the city began on August 21, 1941, when German troops reached the

⊬ Ruins from German bombing raids of Stalingrad, 1942.

southern shore of Lake Ladoga, cutting off Leningrad from land contact with the rest of the Soviet Union.

Hitler ordered that the city and its population of almost three million people be wiped out by bombing, artillery attacks, and starvation. Because Hitler hated Russians and wanted to make an example of the city, even if Leningrad offered to surrender, he would refuse to accept it. During that dreadful winter of 1941–1942, approximately 3,500 to 4,000 Leningrad citizens died of starvation every day.

Because Leningrad is so far north, when winter came, the surface of Lake Ladoga froze solid. In some places the ice was several feet thick. Several hundred thousand people were evacuated from the city across Lake Ladoga via *Doroga Zhizni*, or "Road of Life." This was an "ice road" cleared on the frozen surface of Lake Ladoga that connected the city to unconquered Russian territory just beyond the German lines. Soviet offensives were able to infiltrate the German encirclement, allowing more supplies to reach Leningrad along the shores of Lake Ladoga.

Despite the siege, and the deaths and suffering it caused, the spirit of the citizens of Leningrad remained strong. Composer Dmitry Shostakovich wrote and performed his Seventh Symphony in the besieged city. In January 1943, the Germans were forced back by Soviet army attacks. In January 1944, the siege was lifted. Estimates claim that at least 643,000—and possibly as many as a million—people from Leningrad died before it was over.

In September 1942, Germany began another siege on another important city in the Soviet Union, Stalingrad (now called Vologograd), a city named after Marshal Stalin. It is located on the Volga River less than 250 miles (402 km) northeast of the Caspian Sea. It was another city that Hitler wanted to destroy regardless of the cost. The German Sixth Army of more than 300,000 troops, led by General Friedrich Paulus, was ordered to destroy the city. Instead, on January 31, 1943, it was the Sixth Army that was destroyed. It was a huge victory for the Soviet Union and a crushing defeat for Nazi Germany.

A third huge battle took place in the Soviet Union in the spring of 1943. The German high command saw an opportunity to reverse the series of defeats it had suffered all along the Eastern Front. Soviet advances in the middle of the front had created a large bulge around the city of Kursk. Hitler created a plan, Operation Citadel, to slice through the bulge at its base, cut off the surrounded Soviet troops, and destroy them.

But when Operation Citadel was launched on July 5, 1943, the Soviets were ready. The Battle of the Kursk Salient, as Operation Citadel was also called, ended in another German defeat. With more than 6,000 tanks participating, it was the largest tank battle in World War II.

⊬ Women dig an anti-tank ditch
  in Leningrad, 1942.

OPERATION OVERLORD: D-DAY

The combined American, British, and Canadian invasion of western Europe was the most anticipated event of World War II. General Dwight Eisenhower was appointed head of the Supreme Headquarters Allied Expeditionary Forces (SHAEF) and thus leader of the invasion. The code name of the invasion was Operation Overlord. Helping Eisenhower was a staff that included British general Bernard Montgomery, who would command the ground troops during the invasion; British admiral Bertram Ramsey, who would command the invasion fleet; and British air chief marshal Trafford Leigh-Mallory, who would command the invasion air force.

The invasion site chosen was Normandy, France, opposite the southern coast of England. During the months-long buildup of troops and supplies needed for the invasion, the Allies staged an amazing fake invasion, called Operation Fortitude, to trick the Germans. The goal was to make the Germans think that the invasion would take place farther east, at the French city of Calais, opposite the English city of Dover. Operation Fortitude proved so successful that the German high command continued to believe that Calais was the real invasion site even after Allied troops had landed in Normandy.

MEANWHILE IN THE PACIFIC

On June 19, 1944, the Great Marianas Turkey Shoot is fought between the U.S. and Japanese navies. It ends in a U.S. victory.

Another part of the preparation for D-Day, as Overlord later came to be known, was Eisenhower's "transportation plan." The Allied bombers destroyed the railroad networks and bridges in northern France, Belgium,

✛ Eisenhower talks to paratroopers.

and western Germany. Its purpose was to make it more difficult for the Germans to reinforce troops around Normandy. As it turned out, the Allied air forces did too good of a job. The railroads were so wrecked that not even the Allied troops could use them when they took over the area.

As spring of 1944 approached, Eisenhower came under more and more pressure to decide on a day for the invasion. Many things had to be right for the invasion to succeed. The tides had to be high so the landing craft could safely carry the soldiers over any beach obstacles. There had to be a new moon at night so that there would be little light for the enemy to see the paratroopers who would land behind the beaches. And the weather had to be good—a storm would cause the invasion to be canceled.

In fact, a storm almost did cause the invasion to be canceled. In early June 1944, a violent sea storm hit Normandy. But Eisenhower's weather advisers predicted that a favorable break in the storm would occur the night of June 5 and extend through June 6. Eisenhower thought about it, then gave the signal to go.

In the early-morning hours of June 6, 1944, D-Day was launched with the airborne attack of paratroopers and soldiers transported in gliders. There were five beaches. From east to west, they were code-named Sword (British), Juno (Canadian), Gold (British), Omaha (American), and Utah (American).

For the most part, the British and Canadian troops landed without too much difficulty. But nearby German defenders were swift to counter-attack once they realized what was happening. At times the fighting was desperate, but the British and Canadian forces successfully fought off the Germans and were able to advance inland and, thus, secure the landing site.

Fortune smiled on General Theodore Roosevelt Jr., the leader of the U.S. troops landing on the westernmost D-Day beach of Utah. He was the son of former U.S. President Theodore Roosevelt and a distant cousin of President Franklin Roosevelt. His troops landed south of where they were supposed to, but luck was on their side because their intended landing site was heavily defended. The beach where they landed was lightly held, so they were able to fight their way inland without suffering heavy casualties and quickly link up with the American paratroopers waiting for them.

The story was different at the other American beach of Omaha, located between Utah (on the west) and Gold (on the east). This beach was heavily defended by the Germans. For many hours, it looked as if the Americans, trapped on the beach and unable to move forward, would be wiped out. But eventually the soldiers found ways to break through the German defenses and fight their way inland. The U.S. troops suffered heavy casualties that first day, and they had not managed to fight their way inland as far as their fellow soldiers on the other beaches. But they had carved out their beachhead and were there to stay. At long last, the second front that Stalin had demanded was a reality.

✝ A portion of the troops and supplies landing for Operation Overlord.

The Allied troops in the West were led by some great commanders. Here are a few of the top U.S. and British commanders who fought in France.

General Dwight David Eisenhower

The extremely difficult task of coordinating Allied forces on D-Day, the largest amphibious landing in history, and leading them to victory against Germany was the responsibility of General Dwight Eisenhower. He had proven his ability as the overall leader of Operation Torch, the Allied invasion of northern Africa in 1942, and the later liberation of Sicily in 1943.

In December 1944, he was promoted to the new five-star rank of general of the army. His success as the leader of the Allied troops in the drive across France and into Germany would help him become elected the 34th president of the United States in 1952.

✝ Churchill and Eisenhower in front of London's Guild Hall.

Field Marshal Sir Bernard Law Montgomery

Field Marshal Montgomery was Britain's greatest general in World War II. Montgomery, then a general, served under Eisenhower in 1943 as the commander of the British Eighth Army in the liberation of Sicily.

For Operation Overlord, he again served under Eisenhower, this time as commander of all the ground forces used in D-Day. On August 1, 1944, he was promoted to the rank of field marshal when Eisenhower assumed control of all the ground forces, and Montgomery was made commander of the 21st Army Group, which included all the troops from the British empire. Montgomery led these troops across northern France, Belgium, the Netherlands, and northern Germany. He was knighted on November 11, 1942.

General Omar N. Bradley

General Bradley was the commander of the U.S. First Army during D-Day. After the breakout from Normandy, American forces had grown to include the U.S. Third Army. With two armies now in France, Bradley was promoted to commander of the new 12th Army Group that would initially include the First and Third Armies, and for a time another, the Ninth Army. After the war, General Bradley would be promoted to general of the army and would serve as chairman of the Joint Chiefs of Staff during the Korean War.

General Courtney Hodges

As leader of the U.S. First Army, General Hodges would oversee some of the greatest victories and bloodiest battles in northern Europe. His First Army would liberate Paris, suffer terrible casualties in the Battle of the Hürtgen Forest and the Battle of the Bulge, and seize the Rhine River bridge at Remagen, Germany.

⊬ Omar Bradley in a post-war photograph.

General George S. Patton Jr.

General Patton was one of the ablest and most flamboyant U.S. commanders in World War II. Referred to as "Old Blood and Guts" by his men, Patton distinguished himself as the leader of the American troops landing in northwest Africa in Operation Torch in November 1942. Patton later commanded the U.S. Seventh Army in Sicily.

Later, as the commander of the U.S. Third Army in 1944–45, he helped liberate France, led the dramatic counter-attack against the Germans during the Battle of the Bulge, fought across southern Germany, and, by the end of the war in Europe in May 1945, reached Czechoslovakia.

Patton died tragically in December 1945 as a result of complications suffered in a car accident.

OPERATION COBRA

In the summer of 1944, the Germans were doing their best to hold the American, British, and Canadian forces in Normandy—and they were succeeding. The Germans knew that if any of the forces managed to break through the hedgerow region and reach the open land south and east of Normandy, the German front would collapse. The way would then be open for the Allies to race to Germany.

For weeks after D-Day, bad weather had prevented the Allied air forces from giving much help. Then, on July 18, 1944, American troops captured the key road junction of Saint-Lô, near the southern border of Normandy. The stage was now set for the planned American breakout of Normandy, Operation Cobra.

In Operation Cobra, American bombers would drop tons of bombs just in front of the American soldiers' lines south of Saint-Lô. Then, before the German defenders could recover, the American ground troops would attack and punch a large hole through the defenses. American tanks would then race through the hole and spread out across the open countryside beyond the hedgerows.

MEANWHILE IN THE PACIFIC

On July 21, 1944, U.S. forces land on the island of Guam.

Operation Cobra was launched on July 25, 1944. It was a huge success. The American forces surged out of Normandy in an irresistible flood of tanks and troops. The way to Germany suddenly appeared to be wide open.

✝ (opposite): German POWs captured near Saint-Lô, France.

It was a situation that General George Patton had been dreaming about for a long time. Now in command of the Third Army, he saw a golden opportunity to have his tanks race across the open fields of France and cause panic in the enemy ranks. That's pretty much what happened. General George Patton's Third Army's spectacular drive through France was created by Operation Cobra. On August 1, 1944, General Patton began the operation by ordering his army to move in three directions simultaneously. He thrust one part westward to the French city of Brest, on the tip of the Brittany peninsula. The rest of his army he ordered south and east in a series of broad sweeps to the Loire and Seine Rivers. By September 15, 1944, his troops were deep in eastern France and just a few miles from the German border.

✝ George Patton (left) speaks with "Hap" Arnold (middle), commander of the U.S. Army Air Force, and Mark Clark (right), commander of the American Fifth Army in Italy.

THE LIBERATION OF PARIS

In the summer of 1944, the shattered German army was retreating as fast as it could. On August 19, 1944, Parisians were delighted with news of the impending approach of the Allied armies. It meant their day of liberation from German rule was near. On August 20, Hitler sent an order to his commander in Paris, General Dietrich von Choltitz, to destroy the city. Despite growing pressure from Hitler, von Choltitz made one excuse after another to delay carrying out the order. The truth was, he did not want to go down in history as the man who destroyed one of the greatest cities in the world.

For several days, anarchy swept the city as French Resistance forces launched an insurrection. The Parisians succeeded in taking control of several sections of the city. In those sections, they took revenge against the French people who had collaborated with the Germans.

On August 25, 1944, General von Choltitz surrendered. Finally, Paris was liberated!

✝ French women believed to be Nazi collaborators are marched through the streets of Paris before being turned over to the authorities.

OPERATION MARKET-GARDEN

In September 1944, Field Marshal Montgomery presented General Eisenhower with a plan he claimed would lead to the total defeat of Germany by the end of 1944. The plan was Operation Market-Garden. In it, Montgomery's troops would drive up through Holland, cross the Rhine River at the Dutch town of Arnhem, outflank the main German defenses, which were south of Arnhem, and drive deep into Germany. Once that happened, the Germans would possibly be forced to surrender.

Montgomery's strategy was to use an airborne army (accounting for the "market" part of this plan) composed of British, American, and Polish divisions, in a combination of parachute and glider drops, to seize and hold key bridges along the attack route leading to Arnhem. His ground army (composing the "garden" part of his plan) would then race up the route, dash across the bridges, and, after crossing the last bridge at Arnhem, drive into Germany. The last bridge at Arnhem was the key to the whole plan. Without it, Operation Market-Garden would fail.

It was a bold and risky plan. General Eisenhower gave Montgomery the go-ahead because he wanted to end the war as quickly as possible.

On September 17, 1944, more than 2,000 planes and gliders dropped 16,500 paratroopers and 3,500 troops in gliders near the bridges along the attack route. American paratroopers were assigned two bridges. One bridge was quickly captured. The second was not, because the American troops encountered an unexpected strong German defense around it. There were other problems as well. Counter-attacks by German forces delayed the advance of the British ground troops. And at

MEANWHILE IN THE PACIFIC

On September 15, 1944, U.S. Marines land on the Japanese-held island of Peliliu, east of the Philippines. Its capture is necessary for the planned liberation of the Philippines.

Arnhem, even though the British and Polish paratroopers had succeeded in seizing control of that all-important bridge, their situation was desperate. Heavily armed German units based nearby led a series of powerful counter-attacks. Outnumbered and outgunned, the British and Polish paratroopers would be defeated unless help arrived quickly.

These brave paratroopers at Arnhem fought as best they could to hold the bridge. But help could not reach them in time. On September 21, the survivors were forced to surrender. Ultimately, Operation Market-Garden ended in failure, with the Germans still controlling most of the territory that had been attacked. The end of the war was clearly not going to happen by December 31, 1944.

Even though the German army had won at Arnhem, the German generals knew it was only a temporary victory. The American, British, and Canadian landings in France earlier in 1944 meant they were fighting in a situation they dreaded most: a war on two fronts. German reverses on the Western Front during the summer and fall of 1944 were matched by defeats against the Soviet armies on the Eastern Front. In August, the Soviet armies steamrolled their way through Romania and Bulgaria and into Hungary. In the north, they reached Poland. Though no one could predict when the war would end, the Allies saw that soon, indeed, victory would be theirs.

✠ Bernard Law Montgomery

THE LIBERATION OF ITALY

After Mussolini was ousted as the leader of Italy, leaders of the new Italian government surrendered to the Allies in mid-summer 1943. But the Germans had anticipated this. At the same time as the surrender, German troops seized control, in effect invading their former ally. As a result, American and British troops were forced to invade Italy in September 1943.

The mountainous land of Italy is ideally designed for defense. As elsewhere, the Germans proved themselves master builders of defense fortifications. The American and British troops advanced with frustrating slowness. The Allied troops were stopped about 125 miles (201 km) south of Rome at the formidable row of German defenses known as the Gustav Line.

In an effort to force the Germans to abandon the Gustav Line, the Allies attempted to outflank the Germans by landing troops at the coastal city of Anzio, just 50 miles (80 km) south of Rome. The invasion of Anzio was launched on January 22, 1944. The landing itself was a success. The Germans were caught by surprise. But unfortunately for the Allies, the Germans recovered very quickly, reinforced the high ground around the city of Anzio, and counter-attacked. The result was that the Allies were trapped at Anzio for almost four months. It was not until the middle of May 1944 that the Allies were able to break through the Gustav Line and relieve the troops trapped at Anzio.

Soon after, on June 4, 1944, the Allies liberated Rome. Italy would not be liberated until May 2, 1945, when the last German troops, in northern Italy, surrendered.

(opposite): American troops are photographed in Rome in 1945.

THE BATTLE OF THE HÜRTGEN FOREST

By November 1944, U.S. troops from the First Army had crossed the western border of Germany and entered the Hürtgen Forest. The Hürtgen Forest stretches northeast from the Belgian-German border, and covers an area of about 80 square miles (208 sq km). The largest city near it is the German city of Aachen.

The Hürtgen Forest is densely packed with tall fir trees, thus creating a gloomy and treacherous environment for battle. In the middle of November, troops of the First Army entered the forest and found themselves fighting one of the bloodiest engagements in the First Army's history. The German defenders used the terrain, which was alternatingly frozen and slush filled, with great skill. Because of the thick growth of trees, it was impossible for tanks or warplanes to help the U.S. soldiers.

The battle lasted about three weeks. When it was over, in early December, the First Army had suffered about 28,000 casualties from the fighting itself. Thousands more were hospitalized for trench foot, a disease caused by prolonged exposure to cold and wetness that literally rots the feet.

Despite the terrible cost, the First Army succeeded in taking the Hürtgen Forest. But there was little opportunity to savor the victory. In just a few days, the Germans surprised the Allies with a sudden attack that came to be called the Battle of the Bulge.

(opposite): German prisoners march through the ruins of Aachen to captivity.

BATTLE OF THE BULGE

In September 1944, even though Germany was finding it harder and harder to replace its battlefield losses, and defeat appeared inevitable, Hitler was still looking for ways to turn the tables and win against the Allies. He came up with a secret plan for a surprise attack. It would be launched at a place that was the site of one of his victories in 1940, the Ardennes Forest of Belgium. This time his goal would be to drive a wide wedge between the Allied ranks and seize recently liberated Antwerp, Belgium, which had become a major Allied supply port.

Hitler's generals were skeptical. It looked like a longshot at best. But Hitler was insistent. He recognized that for his attack to succeed, surprise was essential. Somehow he managed to keep the buildup of troops and supplies a total secret from the Allies.

On December 16, 1944, the Germans launched their attack through the Ardennes. The Americans were completely surprised. Also helping the Germans was the fact that the weather was terrible. This forced the Allied air forces to remain on the ground. The Germans managed to create a large gap

that, when seen on a map, looked like a gigantic bulge. So the engagement came to be known as the Battle of the Bulge.

One of the strategically important towns in the battle was the Belgian town of Bastogne, because it was the junction of a network of roads. American troops in Bastogne were surrounded by the powerful German advance. The Germans tried to force the Americans to surrender, saying that their situation was hopeless. But when the surrender demand was handed to the American commander at Bastogne, General Anthony McAuliffe, his reply was a defiant "Nuts!" (No!)

General Patton's Third Army, located south of the bulge, was ordered to attack the Germans and rescue the garrison at Bastogne. On December 26, 1944, the first elements of one of his divisions reached the town.

When the weather cleared and the Allies were able to use their air forces, the German offensive was stopped. By January 16, 1945, the bulge was closed.

✝ U.S. troops crawl through snow during the Battle of the Bulge.

THE CAPTURE OF THE REMAGEN BRIDGE

In early spring 1945, the last natural defense protecting Nazi Germany was the Rhine River. Hitler ordered that all bridges crossing the Rhine were to be blown up if it appeared they were about to fall into Allied hands.

Each Allied commander, from Field Marshal Montgomery to General Hodges to General Patton, hoped to capture one of the bridges. But they knew that doing so would be difficult, if not impossible, as Operation Market-Garden had proven.

On March 7, 1945, General Hodges hit the jackpot when some of his troops captured intact a small railroad bridge over the Rhine in a little German town called Remagen. When he heard what had happened, General Eisenhower excitedly ordered Hodges to get everything he could—tanks, troops, supplies—

> **MEANWHILE IN THE PACIFIC**
>
> On February 19, 1945, U.S. Marines land on Iwo Jima.

across the bridge as fast as possible. He wanted to expand the symbolic victory of capturing the Rhine River bridge into an important tactical victory of driving into Germany.

Hitler was furious when he found out. He had the German officers in charge of the garrison at Remagen court-martialed. He then did everything he could to try to destroy the bridge. But the Americans fought off all the attacks.

The bridge, which had been damaged during the American assault that captured it, finally collapsed on its own. But by that time, the Americans had built a number of other temporary bridges nearby, so it didn't matter.

✠ U.S. troops cross the Rhine River, March 11, 1945.

RHINE RIVER CROSSINGS

Field Marshal Montgomery had a grand plan for crossing the Rhine River. It was Operation Plunder. The press and dignitaries, including Prime Minister Winston Churchill, were on hand to observe this massive assault.

In contrast, General Patton was making plans to get his men across before Montgomery's big event and without all the fanfare. Elements of his army successfully crossed the wide German river on March 22, 1945.

As scheduled, on the night of March 23–24, Operation Plunder was launched. The largest military operation since D-Day, it included a preliminary air bombardment, a smoke screen to hide from the Germans the launching of the assault boats, artillery shelling, and the landing of airborne troops. This time, Montgomery's plan was a spectacular success. In addition to Prime Minister Churchill, General Eisenhower was also present to watch.

With the Rhine breached in a number of places, the end of the war in Germany was now truly in sight.

✠ Army trucks cross the Alexander Patch Heavy Pontoon Bridge over the Rhine River, March 28, 1945.

PATTON'S THIRD-ARMY DRIVE THROUGH GERMANY

† A salt mine in Merkers, Germany, filled with Nazi loot, Reichsbank wealth, and museum paintings.

As the Allied armies in western Europe poured into Germany, more and more German troops decided that it was better to surrender than fight what had to them become a hopeless cause. Patton's Third Army, in particular, found itself rolling through southern Germany with amazing speed. When its advance stopped on May 7, 1945, the day the war in Europe ended, the Third Army was almost at the gates of Prague, Czechoslovakia.

During the Third Army's surge through Germany, it made a colossal discovery. It captured the treasure of the Reichsbank (German national bank) that had been hidden in a salt mine near the city of Merkers. In the tunnels of the mine were stacked tons of gold bars, thousands of bags of money from different countries, art treasures looted from museums and people, and other valuables. The find was so spectacular that General Eisenhower personally visited the mine.

† Dwight Eisenhower, Omar Bradley, and George Patton Jr. inspect stolen art treasures.

In his autobiography, *Mein Kampf*, Adolf Hitler outlined his political philosophy. Among other things, Hitler saw one race, the Aryan (Germanic) race, as being the master race. He felt it was superior in every way to non-Aryan races, particularly the Jews. Hitler's hatred of the Jews was so extreme that after he became Germany's leader in 1933, he embarked on a program that would strip the Jews in Germany of their rights. This program ultimately led to what the Nazis called the "Final Solution"—the annihilation of the Jewish race. This terrible period of history, which lasted until the defeat of Germany in 1945, is known in Yiddish as the Destruction, *Churban*; in Hebrew as the Catastrophe, *Shoah*; and most commonly as the Holocaust.

Though Jews were the primary target of the Nazis' hatred, the Holocaust's victims also included other "inferior"

✝ German citizens are forced to view the bodies of Jewish women, victims of the Holocaust.

races and people, including Gypsies, Slavs, Communists, people with "dangerous" political beliefs, the mentally and physically disabled, and homosexuals.

These people were kept in special fenced-in concentration camps that were worse than any prison imaginable. The victims were kept in overcrowded barracks, starved, used as subjects in unorthodox medical experiments, and forced into slave labor. As if that weren't horrific enough, the Nazis turned many of the concentration camps into extermination camps. By war's end, the Nazis had killed six million Jews and millions of others in the camps.

When the Allies began capturing and liberating the concentration camps, the soldiers were horrified and sickened by the sight. It made them all the more determined to win the war as quickly as possible and bring the people who committed this crime against humanity to justice. Prime Minister Churchill said that the Holocaust was "the greatest and most horrible crime ever committed in the whole history of the world."

✠ One of the first prisoners to be freed from the Wobbelin concentration camp near Berlin, 1945.

THE LINKUP OF AMERICAN AND SOVIET TROOPS

On April 25, 1945, U.S. and Soviet troops had a historic meeting on the Elbe River near Torgau, Germany. This linkup cut Nazi Germany in two. It was a day of great celebration for the Allies, for it meant that the end of the war in Europe was at hand.

While the senior commanding generals held formal celebrations, the common soldiers held wild parties. "It was like the finale of a circus," reported one eyewitness.

One Soviet major cried: *Today is the happiest day in all our lives. The most difficult for us were those days when the Germans were at Stalingrad. Now we meet one another and this is the end of the enemy. Long live your great leader! Long live our great leader!*

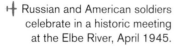 Russian and American soldiers celebrate in a historic meeting at the Elbe River, April 1945.

THE DRIVE TO BERLIN

In early April 1945, the most important city still in Nazi hands was the German capital city of Berlin. All the Allied military leaders wanted to be the first to seize the city. Because the Soviet army had almost reached the eastern suburbs of Berlin, many people thought that the western Allies didn't have a chance.

But the German troops east of Berlin managed to slow the Soviet army advance to a crawl. Meanwhile, troops from the U.S. Ninth Army had reached the Elbe River and were approximately 60 miles (97 km) from Berlin. The Ninth Army's commander, General William Simpson, was certain that his troops could beat the Russians to Berlin. As he was making plans to do just that, he received orders from General Eisenhower to stop at the Elbe and wait for the Russians to link up with him. Simpson did not like the order, but he was a good soldier and he obeyed it. Other people, especially Prime Minister Churchill, thought Eisenhower had made a huge mistake with his order. Churchill said that the capture of Berlin had tremendous symbolic value. Eisenhower said that he was afraid that the advance would needlessly cost thousands of American lives at a time when it was obvious the Allies were going to win. He did not want to pay such a bloody price for such a trophy.

On May 2, 1945, the Soviet army captured Berlin. In less than a week, Germany would surrender.

On May 6, 1945, Hitler's successor, Admiral Karl Doenitz, ordered all German forces to surrender. The next day, May 7, German representatives signed unconditional-surrender documents. However, the Soviet Union refused to recognize the surrender ceremony at Eisenhower's headquarters on May 7, necessitating a second surrender and a separate Soviet V-E Day in Berlin, on May 8. May 8, 1945, was declared V-E Day—"Victory in Europe."

Prime Minister Winston Churchill addressed the British people on May 8, and his speech summarized the feelings of many.

We may allow ourselves a brief period of rejoicing; but let us not forget for a moment the toil and efforts that lie ahead. Japan, with all her treachery and greed, remains unsubdued. . . . We must now devote all our strength and resources to the completion of our task, both at home and abroad.

✛ German representatives sign the unconditional surrender treaty at Rheims, France, on May 7, 1945.

WAR CRIMES TRIALS AT NUREMBERG

After the war in Europe was over, the victorious Allies put into action their plan to bring to trial top Nazi leaders and other select Germans and pro-Nazi collaborators. These people were charged with war crimes, violations of the Geneva Convention, which listed the rules of war and how military prisoners and captured civilians were to be treated; crimes against humanity; and crimes against international peace.

The most important war crimes trials in Europe were held at Nuremberg, Germany. The trials lasted from November 1945 to October 1946. A total of 22 top Nazi leaders, including Admiral Doenitz, were tried at Nuremberg. When it was over, 12 of the Nazi leaders were sentenced to death, 7 received prison sentences, and 3 were acquitted of all charges and set free. There were other war crimes trials in Europe. And after the Allies defeated Japan, separate war crimes trials were held in Tokyo.

War crimes have no statute of limitations. In other words, anyone who committed a war crime can be punished no matter how long ago the crime happened. One of the more famous recent trials occurred in France in 1989—the trial of Klaus Barbie, known as the "Butcher of Lyon."

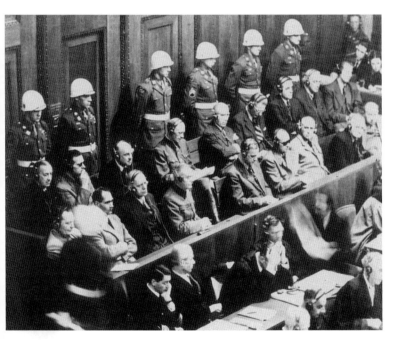

Nazi leaders stand trial at the International War Crimes Tribunal at Nuremberg, Germany.

EPILOGUE: THE MARSHALL PLAN

The war-torn nations of Europe faced famine and economic collapse in the wake of World War II. The only nation strong enough to help the desperate nations was the United States.

On June 5, 1947, at Harvard University, President Truman's secretary of state, George C. Marshall, made one of the most important speeches of the century. Marshall proposed a plan of aid for Europe. He said that the purpose of the plan was to revive the "working economy in the world so as to permit the emergence of political and social conditions in which free institutions can exist." He went on to say, "Our policy is directed . . . against hunger, poverty, desperation, and chaos . . . If we decide to do this thing, I know we can do it successfully. And there's no doubt in my mind that the whole world hangs in the balance."

✛ (opposite): George Marshall

✛ A French farm family receives a tractor courtesy of the Marshall Plan, 1950.

The result of this speech was an economic recovery program that came to be called the Marshall Plan. In addition to putting European nations on the road to recovery, it earned Marshall the Nobel Peace Prize.

Allies—The name for the nations, primarily Great Britain, the United States, the Soviet Union, and France, united against the Axis powers.

Amphibious—Able to operate on land and water.

Axis—The countries, primarily Germany, Italy, and Japan, that fought against the Allies.

Campaign—A series of major military operations designed to achieve a long-range goal.

Capitulation—An agreement of surrender.

Concentration Camp—A fenced and guarded group of buildings designed to hold political prisoners and/or prisoners of war.

Court-martial—Military or naval court that tries persons for offenses under military law.

D-Day—Literally "Day-Day." Originally the code name for the day on which a military offensive is to be launched. Specifically refers to June 6, 1944, the Allied invasion of Normandy, France.

Final Solution—German Chancellor Adolf Hitler's program for the systematic killing of the Jewish race.

Fortifications—A military defensive position.

Garrison—A military post or a group of troops stationed at a particular location.

Hedgerow—Row of high, thickly grown plants.

Insurrection—An act of revolt against civil or military government authority.

Nazi—The acronym for NAtionalsoZIalist, the first word of the official title of Hitler's political party, the Nationalsozialistische Deutsche Arbeiterpartie or NSDAP (National Socialist German Workers' Party).

Outflank—To successfully maneuver around the side of an enemy's position.

Reichsbank—The German national bank.

V-E Day—"Victory in Europe Day." The day when representatives of the German government signed the surrender agreement (May 7, 1945), ending the war in Europe and subsequently celebrated each year on that day.

INDEX